NUCLEAR POWER

Published by Smart Apple Media

1980 Lookout Drive

North Mankato, Minnesota 56003

Design and Production by EvansDay Design

Photographs: Archive (Gleb Garanich, Earl Young),
Jim Baron, Gary Benson, Janet Haas, Tom Myers,
Rainbow (Dan McCoy, Hank Morgan), Unicorn
Stock Photos (Arni Kat, Jim Shippee, John Sohm)

LIBRARY OF CONGRESS CATALOGING-IN-PUBLICATION DATA

Gibson, Diane, 1966–

Nuclear power / by Diane Gibson.

p. cm. — (Sources of energy)

Includes index.

Summary: In simple terms, defines nuclear energy,
how it is created and used, its dangers, and poten-
tial for the future. Includes one simple experiment.

ISBN 1-887068-80-5

1. Nuclear engineering—Juvenile literature.

2. Nuclear energy—Juvenile literature.

[1. Nuclear energy.] I. Title. II. Series.

TK9148 .G53   2000

333.792′4—dc21   99-055893

FIRST EDITION

9 8 7 6 5 4 3 2 1

S O U R C E S   O F   E N E R G Y ::::::::::::::::::::

nuclear power

DIANE GIBSON

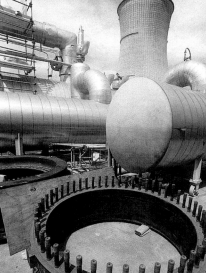

nuclearpower

DEEP IN THE MIDDLE OF A NUCLEAR POWER PLANT, INTENSE HEAT IS CREATED WITHOUT BURNING ANYTHING. AN ATOM FROM A METAL CALLED URANIUM IS BEING SPLIT IN TWO. THE ATOM IS SO TINY THAT IT CANNOT BE SEEN, EVEN WITH A MICROSCOPE. YET AS THE ATOM DIVIDES INTO SMALLER PIECES, A POWERFUL WAVE OF HEAT IS RELEASED. THIS EFFICIENT FORM OF ENERGY IS KNOWN AS NUCLEAR POWER.

SPLITTING ATOMS

⊙ NUCLEAR POWER IS the heated energy from the fission, or splitting, of **atoms**. Splitting atoms is difficult because they are so small. Millions of atoms put together would still be smaller than the dot made by a sharp pencil. Even smaller are the three parts that make up an atom. They are called neutrons, protons, and electrons. The neutrons and protons make up the center, or nucleus, of an atom. Electrons circle around the nucleus. ◎ To split an atom, workers in the power plant use a special machine called a nuclear reactor to shoot electricity-charged neutrons at atoms. When hit correctly, the atom splits into two equal parts, and the neutrons inside are set free. Those neutrons then go on to split other atoms, which release more neutrons, and so on. This sequence is known as a chain reaction. It is like knocking over a row of dominoes.

POWER PLANTS USE MANY
TANKS AND PIPES TO HOLD
AND CARRY THE WATER
HEATED BY ATOMIC FISSION.

EXTRA STEAM PRO-
DUCED IN NUCLEAR
POWER PLANTS IS
RELEASED THROUGH
COOLING TOWERS.

By the year 2001, more than 430 nu-clear power plants were operating around the world. More than a quar-ter of them were in the United States.

MAKING ELECTRICITY

THE CENTER OF a nuclear reactor is called the core. The core looks like a big barrel. Inside it are hollow poles filled with uranium. These poles are called fuel rods. Nuclear fission takes place inside the rods, producing great heat. Water is piped into the core and between the hot rods. This water also becomes very hot—up to 570° F (300° C). Because the water is under pressure in a contained area, it stays in a liquid form and does not turn into steam. When the water gets hot enough, it leaves the core. The heated water is then piped to a machine called a heat exchanger, where it is used to boil a huge tank of water. The boiling water produces steam, which is used to power generators, the machines that create electricity. Wires then carry this electrical power from the plant to homes and other buildings. Outside of nuclear power plants are tall, round buildings called cooling towers. The clouds that rise out of these towers are not smoke, but excess steam from the heat exchanger.

To shield themselves from radiation, people working with nuclear energy wear protective suits.

Most nuclear reactors use uranium for fuel. Others are fueled by plutonium, which is made from the waste generated by other nuclear reactors.

The first large nuclear power plant to produce electricity for people's homes opened in Calder Hall in northwest England in 1956.

POWER PLANT WORKERS
WATCH CAREFULLY TO MAKE
SURE THAT ALL EQUIPMENT
IS WORKING PROPERLY.

NUCLEAR POWER PROBLEMS

WHEN MISHANDLED, NUCLEAR energy can be harmful. It produces radiation—dangerous waves of energy that can hurt or even kill people. These waves can burn skin and leave blisters. Sometimes years go by before people suffer from illnesses caused by exposure to radiation. Reactors need to be carefully monitored. Workers must constantly watch to make sure a meltdown doesn't occur. A meltdown takes place when the uranium fuel becomes so hot that it melts and escapes from the reactor. When this happens, radiation also escapes. This can harm people even miles away. To keep safe, workers in nuclear power plants wear special protective clothing. Often, they also carry machines that test the air. If the machines detect radiation, an alarm goes off. When handling fuel, the workers stay behind thick walls with glass windows. They control **robots** that do the work near the radiation. Nuclear

THE CHERNOBYL POWER PLANT IN UKRAINE WAS SHUT DOWN AFTER A MELTDOWN HAPPENED THERE IN 1986.

waste is the material left after the fuel is used up. Nuclear waste produces radiation, too, so it is stored in special barrels underground. Often, the waste is placed into old salt mines, where it is very dry. If the waste is disposed of where it can get wet, it will spread wherever the water goes.

JOINING ATOMS

NATURE PRODUCES ITS own nuclear power, but it uses a different method called fusion. Fusion takes place when the nuclei of many atoms are joined, or fused, together. The heat and light from the sun are the result of nuclear fusion. When **hydrogen** atoms in the sun fuse together, they change into **helium**. During this change, energy is released in the form of heat and light.   Some day we may use nuclear fusion—rather than fission—to create energy. Nuclear fusion would create less waste and would lessen the chance of releasing dangerous radiation into the atmosphere.   The problem in creating nuclear fusion is that the temperatures required must reach millions of degrees Fahrenheit. This is very hard to do. However, scientists are working on ways to safely generate the heat needed. Many hope to have nuclear fusion reactors making electricity by the year 2030.

NUCLEAR REACTORS
TRIGGER THE FISSION,
RATHER THAN FUSION,
OF ATOMS.

Nuclear power plants last only about 50 years because of the cumulative effects of radiation. Nearly half of the electricity in France and Belgium is produced from nuclear power. About one-sixth of the electricity in Canada and the United States comes from nuclear power.

Nuclear energy is also known as atomic energy. Uranium atoms are used in nuclear fission because they split more easily than other kinds of atoms.

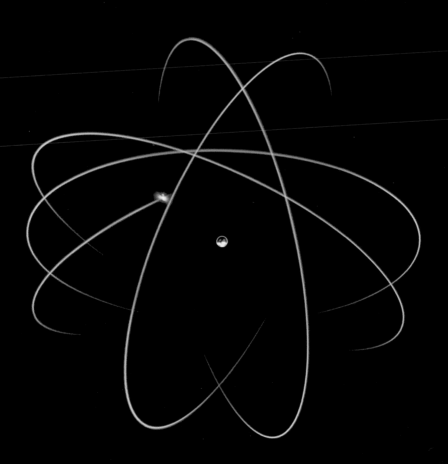

ATOMIC ENERGY IS CREATED WHEN NEUTRONS ARE RELEASED FROM AN ATOM'S NUCLEUS.

THE FUTURE OF NUCLEAR POWER

⊙ NUCLEAR POWER HAS many advantages over other forms of energy. Fuels such as coal and oil must be burned to produce energy. This can release **pollution** into the air. Nuclear power plants, when working properly, do not damage the air. ◎ Also, nuclear power does not require as much fuel as other forms of energy. One pound (373 g) of uranium produces as much energy as 1,500 tons (1,360 t) of coal, or millions of barrels of oil. Scientists are always working on ways to make nuclear power a safer form of energy. With this research, the day may come when most of our energy needs are met by splitting—or even fusing—atoms.

BY PRODUCING STEAM INSTEAD OF SMOKE, NUCLEAR ENERGY IS AMONG THE CLEANEST SOURCES OF POWER.

SCIENTISTS BELIEVE THAT
WE WILL GET MUCH OF OUR
POWER IN THE FUTURE
FROM NUCLEAR ENERGY.

Canada's first nuclear power plant opened in 1962 in Rolphton, Ontario. The first nuclear plant in the United States opened in 1957 in Shippingport, Pennsylvania.

HISTORY

⊙ Since 1955, the United States Navy has used nuclear energy to power submarines and large ships called aircraft carriers. The biggest of these nuclear submarines is the Trident, which weighs 18,000 tons (16,330 t) and is about 560 feet (170 m) long. Nearly all of the submarines used by the Navy are nuclear-powered. ⊚ The largest nuclear-powered aircraft carrier currently in use is the U.S.S. Nimitz. It can hold more than 6,300 people and 100 aircraft. The Nimitz's nuclear reactors allow the huge ship to travel at more than 34 miles (55 km) per hour. Because it uses nuclear energy, the Nimitz can travel up to one million miles (1.6 million km) before it needs to stop to add fuel.

◉ **Splitting Atoms**   Splitting atoms to create nuclear power takes great precision. You can find out if you have what it takes to do the job with this experiment. You will need:

> **A piece of black construction paper**
> **Some sticks of chalk**
> **A small hammer or rock**

⊙ Lay the piece of paper on a flat surface that can't be marred, such as a tile floor. Set a stick of chalk in the middle of the paper.

⊙ Now carefully hit the chalk with the hammer or rock. See if you can divide the stick in half. To be like a properly split atom, the two pieces of chalk must be the same size.

⊙ Check the paper for any dust from the inside of the chalk. The dust is like the neutrons released during fission.

Atoms ARE THE SMALLEST PARTS THAT MAKE UP A SUBSTANCE.

Electricity IS A TYPE OF ENERGY USED IN HOMES TO RUN LIGHTS AND APPLIANCES.

Helium AND **hydrogen** ARE BOTH COLORLESS GASES.

Pollution IS HARMFUL MATERIALS THAT MAKE AIR OR WATER DIRTY.

Robots ARE MACHINES THAT ARE GUIDED BY HUMANS TO DO VARIOUS KINDS OF WORK.